THE STORY OF THE NEW ORLEANS PELICANS

Chris Paul

Zion Williamson

A HISTORY OF HOOPS
THE STORY OF THE

NEW ORLEANS PELICANS

JIM WHITING

CREATIVE SPORTS

Anthony Davis

CREATIVE EDUCATION / CREATIVE PAPERBACKS

Published by Creative Education and Creative Paperbacks
P.O. Box 227, Mankato, Minnesota 56002
Creative Education and Creative Paperbacks are imprints of
The Creative Company
www.thecreativecompany.us

Design and production by Blue Design (www.bluedes.com)
Art direction by Rita Marshall

Photographs by Corbis (Steve Lipofsky), Getty (Jonathan Bachman, Nathaniel
S. Butler, Ronald Cortes, James Drake, Focus On Sport, Chris Graythen, Kent
Homer, Harry How, John Iacono, Alika Jenner, Jacob Kupfeman, David Liam
Kyle, Fernando Medina, Manny Millan, Layne Murdoch, Joe Murphy, Bob
Rosato, Gregory Shamus), Icon Sports Media Inc. (Albert Pena/Icon SMI),
© Steve Lipofsky, Newscom (Mike Brown, Ron Jenkins, Ting Shen/Xinhua/
Photoshot), USPresswire (David Butler II)

Library of Congress Cataloging-in-Publication Data
Names: Whiting, Jim, 1943- author.
Title: The story of the New Orleans Pelicans / By Jim Whiting.
Description: Mankato, Minnesota : Creative Education and Creative
    Paperbacks, [2023] | Series: Creative Sports: A History of Hoops |
    Includes index. | Audience: Ages 8-12 |
    Audience: Grades 4-6 | Summary: "Middle grade basketball fans are
    introduced to the extraordinary history of NBA's New Orleans Pelicans
    with a photo-laden narrative of their greatest successes and losses"--
    Provided by publisher.
Identifiers: LCCN 2022016847 (print) | LCCN 2022016848 (ebook) | ISBN
    9781640266353 (library binding) | ISBN 9781682771914 (paperback) | ISBN
    9781640007765 (pdf)
Subjects: LCSH: New Orleans Pelicans (Basketball team)--History--Juvenile
    literature. | New Orleans Pelicans (Basketball
    team)--Biography--Juvenile literature.
Classification: LCC GV885.52.N376 W56 2022 (print) | LCC GV885.52.N376
    (ebook) | DDC 796.323/640976335--dc23
LC record available at https://lccn.loc.gov/2022016847
LC ebook record available at https://lccn.loc.gov/2022016848

Jaxson Hayes

CONTENTS

LEGENDS OF THE HARDWOOD

Zion Williamson

After a sensational freshman season at Duke University, 18-year-old 6-foot-6 power forward Zion Williamson was the first overall choice in the 2019 NBA (National Basketball Association) Draft by the New Orleans Pelicans. Unfortunately, he suffered a serious knee injury before the season began. He finally made his debut on January 22, 2020 against the San Antonio Spurs. A sellout crowd jammed Smoothie King Center in New Orleans even though the team was 10 games under .500.

Williamson was quiet in the first three quarters. He lived up to his hype in the fourth quarter. Over a six-minute span, he scored all 17 of his team's points. He finished with 22 points in a total of 18 minutes. That is the highest point total in NBA history for anyone in his first game while playing less than 20 minutes. Williamson also went 4-for-4 from 3-point range. It was the first time a player had done that in his debut.

His assault on the record book was just getting started. Four games after his debut, Williamson had 24 points in a blowout win over the Memphis Grizzlies. He scored 21, 20, and 21 in his next three games.

Then he really hit his stride. He averaged 29 points in the following four games. On February 24, he scored 29 points against the Los Angeles Lakers. That matched a record that then-19-year-old Denver Nuggets rookie Carmelo Anthony had set

P.J. Brown

PAST MEETS PRESENT

UTAH JAZZ VS. NEW ORLEANS HORNETS
OCTOBER 30, 2002

The NBA returned to New Orleans for the first time since
April of 1979. The city's new team hosted its old franchise.
The game had some Louisiana themes. Louisiana natives
scored the first two baskets of the game. Utah's Karl Malone
and New Orleans's P.J. Brown did the honors. Both played
collegiately at Louisiana Tech. At halftime, the Hornets
honored a local Louisiana hero. "Pistol Pete" Maravich
starred at Louisiana State University. He set a still-standing
college career average of 44.2 points per game. He was the
cornerstone of the Jazz roster when the franchise began
in New Orleans in 1974. The Hornets retired Maravich's No.
7 jersey at halftime. New Orleans guard Baron Davis did his
best Maravich impression scoring 21 points and adding 10
assists. The Hornets routed the Jazz, 100-75.

in the 2003–04 season. Anthony had a streak of nine games in which he scored at least 20 points. He was the first teenager to record that feat.

Four days later, Williamson's 24 points against the Cleveland Cavaliers marked a new teenage record of 10 games. He wouldn't turn 20 for several months. The streak reached 13 before finally ending on March 6. The Miami Heat held him to just 17 points. CBS television writer Brad Botkin summed up what he had done: "Williamson continues to take the NBA by storm with a combination of athleticism, power and force that has rarely, if ever, been seen—certainly not in a teenager... Gigantic, athletically elite grown men have absolutely no idea what to do with him."

That group of elite grown men included Lakers superstar LeBron James. He had faced Williamson twice during that 13-game span. The rookie actually outscored him the second time, notching 35 points to James's 34. "You have to actually be out on the floor to actually feel the strength and the speed that he plays at," James said.

The NBA's history in New Orleans dates back nearly 50 years before Williamson burst onto the scene. The league granted the city an expansion franchise in 1974. Team officials named the new team the Jazz. "Jazz is one of those things for which New Orleans is nationally famous and locally proud," said co-owner Fred Rosenfeld. "It is a great art form which belongs to New Orleans and its rich history."

Unfortunately, the Jazz didn't make sweet music on the court. They won just 23 games in their first season even though they had traded for local hero Pete Maravich. Four more losing seasons followed. Fans lost interest. In 1979, the team moved to Salt Lake City, Utah. It kept the Jazz name even though their new home was far more famous for the Mormon Tabernacle Choir, which featured a very different kind of music.

Many people in New Orleans wanted to replace the Jazz with another team. They finally had an opportunity in 1994. A local group offered to buy the Minnesota Timberwolves. The deal fell apart at the last minute. Seven years later, the Vancouver Grizzlies wanted to move. New Orleans made a bid for the team. So did three other cities. The Grizzlies chose Memphis, Tennessee.

THE HORNETS BUZZ INTO NEW ORLEANS

At the same time that the Grizzlies were moving to Memphis in 2001, the Charlotte Hornets were also looking for a new home. They had had the league's worst attendance in the 2001–02 season. Owner George Shinn demanded that the city build a new arena at no cost to him. He said he couldn't afford to keep the team in Charlotte without one. The city refused. New Orleans still wanted an NBA team. The third time proved to be the charm. The Hornets headed to the "Big Easy," as the city is often called.

The Hornets' first game in their new home in the 2002–03 season was a combination of past and present. They faced the Utah Jazz. The Hornets swarmed all over the Jazz, winning 100–75. Point guard Baron Davis and small forward Jamal Mashburn become fan favorites during the season. The Hornets finished 47–35. They lost to the Philadelphia 76ers in the first round of the playoffs.

Baron Davis

After going 41-41 the following season, the Hornets began 2004–05 by losing 29 of their first 31 games. They improved during the rest of the season but still finished with just 18 wins. It was the worst record in the team's history. The poor record meant the team had a high pick in the 2005 NBA Draft. They took point guard Chris Paul. "He has great leadership skills," said general manager Allan Bristow. "We feel he can be a part of an explosive young backcourt for us." Unfortunately, it would be three years before fans in New Orleans got to see him play. Nature was about to let loose its fury on the city.

A month before the start of the 2005–06 season, Hurricane Katrina pummeled New Orleans and the surrounding area. Almost 2,000 people died. Massive floods put nearly 80 percent of the city under several feet of water. The Hornets couldn't

P.J. Brown at opening jump ball

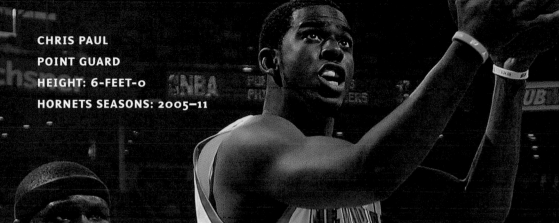

CHRIS PAUL
POINT GUARD
HEIGHT: 6-FEET-0
HORNETS SEASONS: 2005–11

LEGENDS
OF THE HARDWOOD

GRANDFATHER

Chris Paul's grandfather, Nathaniel Jones, owned a service station in North Carolina. He loved watching Paul's high school games. He always closed early on those days. In 2002, Jones was beaten to death. He was 61. Paul's aunt suggested that he should try to score 61 points in his next game, one point for every year of Jones's life. Paul reached his goal by scoring a lay-up with less than two minutes left. He was fouled on the play. "I walked to the free throw line, [the referee] gave me the ball and I shot an air ball right out of bounds," Paul said. He left the game and started crying. He'd honored his grandfather.

LEGENDS
OF THE HARDWOOD

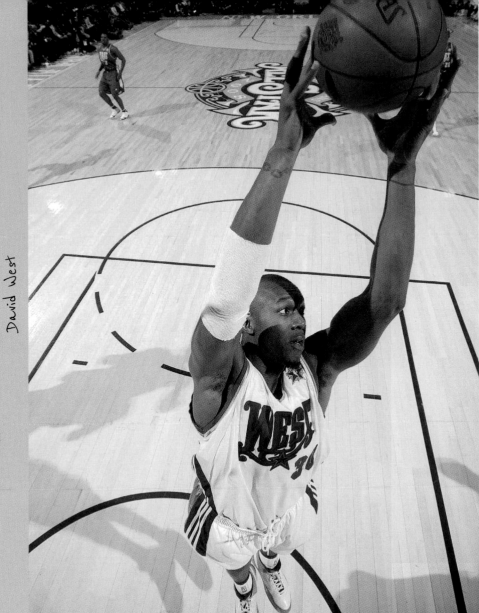

David West

NBA ALL-STAR GAME
NEW ORLEANS
FEBRUARY 17, 2008

THE STARS SHINE ON NEW ORLEANS

The NBA wanted to help New Orleans recover from Hurricane Katrina. So the
league scheduled the 2008 All-Star Game in the city. "I think the game helped
New Orleans," said Sacramento Kings coach George Karl. Hornets fans were
thrilled that point guard Chris Paul and power forward David West both played
in the game. Paul scored 16 points, dished out 14 assists, and had 4 steals.
West netted six points. Both players also joined community service projects
during the All-Star weekend. "It was something that really put basketball in
perspective," said West. "It made us realize how real life can be."

play their home games in New Orleans. They relocated to Oklahoma City. The city had built the Ford Center in 2002 to be ready if the NBA gave them a team. Paul lived up to expectations. He led all rookies in scoring, assists, steals, total minutes played, double-doubles, and triple-doubles. He was the runaway winner of the NBA Rookie of the Year award. The Hornets improved to 38 wins but missed the playoffs.

New Orleans still hadn't recovered from Katrina in time for the 2006–07 season. The Hornets stayed in Oklahoma City. They missed the playoffs again. That didn't matter to fans. They were enthusiastic about "their" team. Many people, including coach Byron Scott, wanted the Hornets to stay there permanently. "I think our guys are at home here," Scott said. But the NBA didn't think it was a good idea. If the Hornets stayed in Oklahoma City, people might think the league was deserting the hard-hit city of New Orleans. It would create bad publicity.

BACK TO THE BIG EASY

The Hornets returned to New Orleans for the 2007–08 season. Players such as forward Peja Stojakovic and center Tyson Chandler provided scoring and defense. The Hornets buzzed to a franchise-best 56–26 mark. Scott was voted NBA Coach of the Year. New Orleans easily defeated the Dallas Mavericks in the first round of the playoffs, 4 games to 1. They took a 3–2 series lead in the second round over the defending NBA champion Spurs. But San Antonio won the two final games to take the series.

New Orleans stayed on the winning track the following year. They won 49 games and faced Denver in the first round of the playoffs. The Nuggets won the series, 4 games to 1. Chandler was traded before the 2009–10 season. Paul was injured for half the season. The Hornets finished with a disappointing 37–45 mark.

New Orleans rebounded to win 46 games the following season. Once again, they lost in the first round of the playoffs. The biggest news happened off the court. For the second time in less than a decade, Shinn was having financial problems. He wanted to sell the team. One potential buyer wanted to move it to California. The NBA refused to approve the sale. A local man made an offer, but it fell through. The league decided to buy the team itself and keep it in New Orleans.

The 2011–12 season started late because of disputes about money between owners and players. Paul was traded to the Los Angeles Clippers. Leaving the team was hard. "I was really a part of that city," Paul said. "I honestly can't say one negative thing about the city. If it were not for the city of New Orleans, I'm not who I am now. They just embrace you as family." Without their best player, the Hornets struggled to a 21–45 mark.

Marcus Thornton

ANTHONY DAVIS
POWER FORWARD/CENTER
HEIGHT: 6-FOOT-10
HORNETS/PELICANS SEASONS: 2012–19

UNDER THE RADAR

In high school, Anthony Davis played for Perspectives Charter School in Chicago. The academic-driven school didn't even have a gym. Most people dismissed him as "the little guy who would shoot threes from the corner." That was fine with him. "I wasn't going there because of basketball," Davis said. "My dream was always to go to college." Then he started growing. By his senior year, he stood 6-foot-10. He starred on a traveling club team. Suddenly, college teams were interested in him. Davis realized his dream when he received a scholarship to the University of Kentucky. In his first year, he led the Wildcats to the national championship. He was named College Player of the Year.

FROM HORNETS TO PELICANS

I n 2012, New Orleans businessman Tom Benson bought the team. He also owned the New Orleans Saints of the National Football League. "There was concern by Mr. Benson that someone outside would buy this franchise [the Hornets] and try to move it and, to be quite honest, that was not what we wanted to do because we had invested so much in this community," said team president Dennis Lauscha. Benson didn't like the Hornets name. He said it had no connection with New Orleans. He wanted something with more of a local flavor.

He offered to buy the Jazz name from Utah. A Salt Lake City newspaper columnist wrote, "I can't understand why we don't let him have it." He pointed out that the team colors of green, purple, and gold had been the official colors of the Mardi Gras Festival in New Orleans since 1892. Utah owner Greg Miller replied, "We are Jazz. And we always will be." The team had more than 30 years of history as the Jazz. It would also be expensive to redesign the team's merchandise.

Benson chose Pelicans instead. The brown pelican is the state bird of Louisiana. New Orleans sports historian S. Derby Gisclair added that the name is "very emblematic because several years ago, brown pelicans were almost extinct. They made a comeback. New Orleans, after Hurricane Katrina, made its comeback."

In 2004, Charlotte had acquired a new team called the Bobcats. But the city had always had a fondness for the Hornets name. Teams in several sports had used it.

J.R. Smith

The NBA made a deal. New Orleans would become the Pelicans in 2013. Then Charlotte would take back the Hornets name. Charlotte would also reclaim the team's history between its 1988 founding and moving to New Orleans. Accordingly, the Pelicans' official NBA history began with the 2002–03 season.

As Benson was finalizing the sale, the team's future arrived: that was burly power forward/center Anthony Davis. "AD" had had a sensational freshman year at the University of Kentucky. New Orleans took him as the top overall choice in the 2012 NBA Draft. "New Orleans is a great city," Davis said. "When I came in, whatever I had to do to make everything go positively, I was more than willing and happy to do."

In his first season, Davis scored 13.5 points and snagged 8 rebounds a game. He was named to the NBA All-Rookie First Team. The Pelicans, though, weren't as successful. They won only 27 games that season and 34 in the following one.

Tyson Chandler

JRUE HOLIDAY
POINT/SHOOTING GUARD
HEIGHT: 6-FOOT-3
PELICANS SEASONS: 2013–20

JRUE JAMES INTO THE RECORD BOOK—TWICE!

On January 29, 2019, Jrue Holiday set a new NBA record when he had 19 points, 6 rebounds, and 6 blocked shots. He became the first guard to record those numbers in a game. He was especially proud of the blocked shots. "It's my inner Anthony [Davis], man," he said. He bookended the year on December 28 when he and his brothers Justin and Aaron—both of them Indiana Pacers—became the first trio of brothers to be on the same court at the same time. New Orleans romped to a 120–98 win. "It was cool," Holiday said. "I beat 'em and I got their jerseys."

ONE STAR LEAVES, ANOTHER ARRIVES

The Pelicans returned to the winning column in 2014–15 with 45 wins. By then it was obvious that AD would be one of the league's biggest stars. He was scoring well over 20 points and hauling in 10 rebounds a game. The Pelicans played Golden State in the first round of the playoffs. The eventual NBA champion Warriors swept the series. New Orleans couldn't build on that success. The team won just one of its first 12 games in 2015–16. It finished 30–52.

The Pelicans had high hopes for center DeMarcus Cousins. He joined the team in a late-season trade in 2016–17. He arrived too late to salvage the season. It was a different story in 2017–18. Cousins and Davis formed a formidable front line. In January, Cousins had 44 points, 24 rebounds, and 10 assists against the Chicago Bulls. He was just the 10th player in league history with that 40/20/10 line. But he tore his Achilles tendon four days later and was lost for the season. The team still won 48 games. And for the only second time in franchise history, the Pelicans won a first-round playoff series. They swept the Portland Trail Blazers. But they lost to the Warriors in the next round.

Cousins didn't return for the 2018–19 season. New Orleans fell back, winning just 33 games. Davis asked the team to trade him to the Lakers. He wanted to win a championship and didn't feel the Pelicans provided that opportunity. New Orleans received three good young players and several draft picks. Newcomer

BRANDON INGRAM
POWER/SMALL FORWARD
HEIGHT: 6-FOOT-8
PELICANS SEASONS: 2019-PRESENT

IT PAYS TO HAVE GOOD FRIENDS

Brandon Ingram's father Donald wanted to play in Europe. It didn't work out, but he taught his son to play basketball. Donald made another contribution to his son's development: He was a longtime friend of former NBA star Jerry Stackhouse. Stackhouse mentored Ingram. What Ingram learned helped his high school team win the state title all four years he played. The Lakers made him the second overall draft pick in 2016. Ingram came to the Pelicans as part of the Anthony Davis trade. New Orleans proved to be a perfect fit. Ingram had averaged 14 points per game with the Lakers. As a Pelican, his average soared to 23 points per game. He was named the NBA Most Improved Player and played in the All-Star Game.

NEW ORLEANS PELICANS

Devonte' Graham

Brandon Ingram took up some of scoring slack after Davis's departure. But even with the arrival of Zion Williamson, the Pelicans struggled. They won just 30 games that season and 31 in 2020–21.

Williamson missed the entire 2021–22 season due to injury. The Pelicans lost 12 of their first 13 games. They played at the .500 level during the rest of the season. They finished 36–46. That was ninth in the Western Conference. They defeated the Spurs and Clippers in the play-in tournament to qualify for the playoffs. They faced Phoenix in the first round. Many people thought that Phoenix would sweep the best-of-seven series. The Suns won 64 games during the season. They easily won Game 1. Moments before the trade deadline in February, the Pelicans had traded for shooting guard C.J. McCollum. He and Ingram led New Orleans to a victory in Game 2. The Pelicans nearly won Game 3 as well, losing by just three points. They won Game 4. The Suns took the next two games to win the series. "The future is very bright," said McCollum. "We'll have an all-world player [Williamson] coming next year." To hopefully go along with their bright future, New Orleans selected guard Dyson Daniels with the eighth pick in the 2022 NBA Draft.

The Pelicans have survived shaky ownership and several moves. They weathered one of the worst natural disasters in American history. Now they have put down solid roots. Fans hope that the team will soon do what the Saints have already done: bring a championship trophy to the Big Easy.

C.J. McCollum

INDEX